# THE STEADFAST TIN SOLDIER

**12** 장난감 병정

*Hans Christian Andersen*

Adapted by **Lori Olcott**
Illustrated by **Kim Sook**

Copyright © WORLDCOM 2003

Published in Korea in 2003 by WORLDCOM

All rights reserved. No part of this publication may be reproduced, stored in a retrieval system, or transmitted in any form or by any means, electronic, mechanical, photocopying, recording, or otherwise, without the prior written permission of the publisher.

Printed and distributed by WORLDCOM

# 작가와 작품 설명

안델센(Hans Christian Andersen, 1805 ~ 75)은 덴마크의 가난한 가정에서 태어나 제대로 배우지도 못했으나, 어릴 적부터 문학에 눈을 떴다. 생활이 곤란한 형편이었으나, 문학에의 간절한 소망과 타고난 소질, 그리고 소박하고 순진한 성격으로 많은 후원자를 찾아냈다. 1833년 이탈리아 여행의 인상과 체험을 바탕으로 창작한 『즉흥시인』으로 그의 이름이 유럽 전체에 퍼졌다. 같은 해에 내놓은 최초의 『동화집』은 그의 동화작가로서의 생애의 출발점이 되었다. 그의 동화의 특색은 서정적인 정서와 아름다운 환상의 세계, 그리고 따스한 휴머니즘으로 정리할 수 있다.

주요 작품으로는 『미운 오리 새끼』 『벌거벗은 임금님』 『인어공주』 등이 있고 모두 130편 이상의 주옥같은 책을 펴냈다.

### 작품 설명

『안데르센 동화』는 작가 자신이 스스로 고뇌하며 창작한 문학 작품으로 인생의 여러 주제를 다루어 자신의 불우한 환경과 고통을 은연중에 반영하거나 그것을 승화시키고자 했다. 이 작품의 외다리 장난감 병정 또한 소외감과 열등의식에 시달리는 안데르센 자신을 표현하고 있다. 비록 장난감 병정과 춤추는 인형의 사랑이 죽음으로써 이루어지는 슬픈 내용이지만, 어린이들에게 용기와 헌신적인 사랑을 일깨워 주는 작품이라 하겠다.

# Introduction

Hello, and thank you for your interest in Worldcom's Story House! I hope you and your children enjoy the stories and characters we present to you here.

These Fairy tales have been passed down from parent to child for generations and generations. They usually teach a lesson. They teach the values that are important in every culture; like being kind, generous and helpful to others. They show that looks can be deceiving. Something beautiful, can be cruel and evil. But something ugly, can be good and loving. They also teach the value of patience. Rewards for good deeds don't always come quickly. But be patient, and the good deeds you do will bring good deeds to you. And if you keep working hard, your efforts will pay off.

I have tried my best to re-tell these stories in modern and natural English, without being too complicated or too hard. Most middle school children can read these stories. But I hope that parents and other adults will enjoy reading these books with their children too. There are interesting parts in each story. I hope there is enough that everyone will enjoy reading the story and listening to the native speakers.

Again, thank you for joining us in Story House. We hope you enjoy your stay.

# 이 책을 펴내며

안녕하세요. 월드컴의 Story House에 오신 것을 환영합니다. 부디 여러분과 여러분의 자녀들이 이 책이 들려주는 이야기들을 만끽하시길 바랍니다.

이 동화들은 부모에서 아이들에게로 여러 세대에 걸쳐 전해내려 온 이야기로서 교훈을 담고 있습니다. 이웃에게 친절하고 서로 도우면서 아낌없이 베푸는 것, 이러한 가치관의 중요성을 일깨워 주죠. 이러한 것들은 때때로 반대로 표현되기도 합니다. 겉보기에는 아름답지만 잔인하고 사악할 수 있으며, 비록 흉칙하게 보여도 착하고 사랑을 베푸는 사람일 수 있다는 것입니다. 이러한 이야기들은 우리에게 인내의 가치를 일깨워 주기도 합니다. 선한 행동의 대가는 그 즉시 되돌아오지 않습니다. 그러나 참고 기다린다면, 여러분의 선한 행동은 보답을 받을 것입니다. 그리고 열심히 노력한다면 그에 상응하는 결과를 얻을 것입니다.

저는 이 이야기들을 너무 복잡하거나 어렵지 않도록 현대적이고 자연스러운 영어로 전달하기 위해 최선을 다했습니다. 이 책은 중학교 수준의 학생이라면 누구든지 읽을 수 있습니다. 그러나 부모님을 비롯한 모든 이들이 자녀분들과 함께 이 책을 즐길 수 있기를 바랍니다. 이야기마다 제각기 재미있는 부분들이 있습니다. 네이티브들이 들려주는 생생한 이야기는 현장감을 더해 주어 자신도 모르는 사이에 동화세계에 빠져들게 될 것임을 믿어 의심치 않습니다.

다시 한 번 저희 Story House에 오신 것을 감사드리며, 계속 많은 사랑 부탁드립니다.

Lori Olcott

# 등장인물 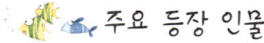 주요 등장 인물

### 장난감 병정
양철로 만들어진 외다리 인형임에도 불구하고 책임감 있고 용감한 병정. 발레리나 인형을 사랑하지만 헤어지게 된다.

### 조니
생일 선물로 받은 장난감 병정을 소중히 여기나 '도깨비 인형'에게 이용당하고 만다.

### 춤추는 인형
아름다운 발레리나 인형. '도깨비 인형'의 협박에도 굴하지 않고 장난감 병정을 헌신적으로 사랑한다.

### 도깨비 인형
수수께끼 상자 속의 인형으로, 장난감 병정을 시기하여 온갖 못된 짓을 꾀한다.

그 외의 등장 인물

 조니의 부모님
(스미스 부부)

광대 인형

 동네 꼬마와 어부들

요리사와 하녀

  들쥐와 물고기

존슨 부부

# Contents

**Chapter 1**   10

**Chapter 2**   18
Comprehension Checkup I   32

**Chapter 3**   36
Comprehension Checkup II   48

## Chapter 4    52
   Comprehension Checkup III    74

## Chapter 5    78
   Comprehension Checkup IV    100

## Answers    104
## Word List    108

# Chapter 1

Once upon a time, there was a little boy. He lived with his parents in a big city. One day, it was his birthday. He woke up and ran down the stairs.

Good morning, Mama.
Good morning, Papa.

Good morning, Johnnie. Happy birthday!

once upon a time  옛날 옛적에
little  조그만, 작은
live with  …와 함께 살다
one day  어느 날
birthday  생일
wake(-woke-waken) up  깨어나다

run(-ran-run) down  뛰어 내려가다
Good morning  (아침 인사)
   안녕하세요
Mama  엄마
Papa  아빠

He woke up and ran down the stairs.
소년은 깨어나서 층계를 뛰어 내려갔습니다.

Good morning, Johnnie. Happy birthday!
안녕, 조니. 생일 축하한다!

- How is my birthday boy?
- Great! I'm six years old today.
- Yes, you are. Do you want to open your presents?
- Yes, please.
- Here you are, son. Just for you.
- Wow! Tin soldiers! Thank you, Papa!
- You're welcome, son.

great 좋은, 굉장한, 멋진
today 오늘
want to …하기를 원하다
open 열다
present 선물

here you are (물건을 내주면서)
　　자, 여기 있어요, 이거 받아요
just 오직, 단지
You're welcome 천만에요

How is my birthday boy?
생일을 맞은 우리 아들 기분은 어떠니?

Here you are, son. Just for you.
이거 받거라, 아들아. 네 것이란다.

They're great! Oh, wait. This one only has one leg.

Hmm, you're right. The tinsmith ran out of tin. I will take him back to the store. We can get a new one for you.

No, I like him. He was hurt in the war. He's the bravest soldier of them all.

Johnnie got many presents for his birthday. But the tin soldiers were his favorite toys. He played with them all day long.

I will take him back to the store. We can get a new one for you.
내가 그 인형을 도로 가게로 가지고 가마. 새 것으로 바꿀 수 있을 테니.

He's the bravest soldier of them all.
이들 중에서 가장 용감한 군인이에요.

Oh, wait 아, 잠깐만요
leg 다리
right 옳은, 맞는
tinsmith 양철공
run(-ran-run) out of
　…을 다 써 버리다, 바닥이 나다
tin 양철, 주석
take back 도로 가져가다
to the store 가게로

get 얻다
hurt 다치다
in the war 전쟁에서
bravest (brave의 최상급)가장 용감한
soldier 군인
favorite 마음에 드는, 매우 좋아하는
toy 장난감
play with …을 가지고 놀다
all day long 하루 종일

Finally, it was time to go to bed.

Bang, bang! Oh no! I'm hit! Here comes the one-legged soldier. He saved us. Hooray!

Are you still playing with your soldiers? Come on, Johnnie, it's bed time for you.

But Mama, we're fighting a war. The teddy bears stole the zoo animals, and the soldiers have to save them.

The soldiers can save the zoo animals tomorrow. You must go to bed now.

Can I play for ten more minutes?

No, it's late. Let's go brush your teeth.

Oh, alright. Good night, tin soldier. Guard the play room. I'll see you tomorrow.

It is time to …할 시간이다
bang (의성어)탕
hit 맞다
one-legged 다리가 하나인, 외다리의
save 구하다
Hooray! 만세
Come on 자, 어서
bed time 잠잘 시간
fight 싸우는

teddy bear 곰인형
steal(-stole-stolen) 훔치다
have to(=must) …해야 한다
zoo 동물원
animal 동물
late 늦은
brush one's teeth 이를 닦다
alright(=all right) 알았어요
guard 지키다, 사수하다

Finally, it was time to go to bed. 마침내, 잠잘 시간이 되었습니다.

Are you still playing with your soldiers?
너 아직도 병정놀이하고 있는 거니?

Can I play for ten more minutes? 10분만 더 놀면 안 될까요?

# Chapter 2

Johnnie and his family went to sleep. The house was quiet. Now the toys woke up to play. Johnnie had many, many toys. They all started to talk and play together. But not the one-legged tin soldier. He had a job to do. He had to guard the play room. A stuffed clown saw the tin soldier. He walked over and introduced himself.

 Hi there. Welcome to the play room. Come play with us.

 Hello, clown. Sorry, I cannot play with you. I must guard the play room.

He had a job to do. 그는 해야 할 일이 있었습니다.
He walked over and introduced himself.
광대는 병정에서로 다가가서 자신을 소개했습니다.

go(-went-gone) to sleep 잠들다
quiet 조용한
wake(-woke-waken) up 깨다
many 많은
start to …하기 시작하다
talk 말하다, 이야기하다
play together 함께 놀다

job 일
stuff 솜을 넣다, 채워 넣다
clown 광대
see(-saw-seen) 보다
walk over …에게로 걸어가다
introduce 소개하다
welcome 환영하다

🤡 Why do you only have one leg? What happened to you?

💂 The tinsmith ran out of tin. But I am still a strong and brave soldier.

🤡 Oh, I see. Do you have any questions about the play room? I know everyone here.

💂 Yes, I have a question. Who is the doll by the toy castle?

🤡 By the toy castle? Oh, her! She is the dancing doll. When her music plays, she dances on her toes.

💂 She is so beautiful. She looks like she only has one leg, just like me.

happen 생기다, 일어나다
tinsmith 양철공
run(-ran-run) out of
　…을 다 써 버리다, 바닥이 나다
strong 힘센, 강한
brave 용감한
question 질문
know 알다

everyone 모두, 모든 사람
doll 인형
toy castle 장난감 성
music 음악
play 연주하다
dance 춤추다
toe 발가락
look like …인 것 같다

When her music plays, she dances on her toes.
음악이 연주되면 그녀는 발끝으로 서서 춤을 추지.

She looks like she only has one leg, just like me.
그녀도 나처럼 한 쪽 다리만 있는 것 같군.

It was true. The dancing doll was a ballerina. She stood on one tip-toe. Her other leg was high behind her back. The tin soldier did not see her other leg. She wore a pretty white ballet dress with a silver star on it.

 I am in love with her.

 Be careful, tin soldier. The Jack-in-the-box loves her too. He is very jealous and very mean. Everyone is afraid of him.

 I am a brave soldier. I am not afraid of the Jack-in-the-box.

Her other leg was high behind her back.
그녀의 다른 쪽 다리는 등 뒤로 높이 올라가 있었습니다.
Everyone is afraid of him.  모두가 그를 두려워한다구.

The Steadfast Tin Soldier

true 진실인
ballerina 발레리나
stand(-stood-stood) 서다
tip-toe 엄지 발가락
behind …의 뒤에
back 등
wear(-wore-worn) 입고 있다
pretty 예쁜
ballet dress 발레복

be in love with …에게 반하다
　　　　　　　　…을 사랑하다
careful 조심스러운
jack-in-the-box 뚜껑을 열면
　인형이 튀어나오는 장난감
jealous 질투가 많은
mean 비열한, 심술궂은
be afraid of …을 두려워하는
brave 용감한

The stuffed clown walked away. Then, the dancing doll called to him.

Clown, who were you talking to?

He is a tin soldier. Johnnie got him for his birthday today.

Why does he only have one leg?

The tinsmith ran out of tin.

He looks so brave and handsome. Ask him to come here.

He will not come here. He says he must guard the play room. But he saw you. He says you are very beautiful.

He does? How wonderful. I wish he would come here and talk to me. But we can only look at each other.

walk away 떠나가다
call to …을 부르다
talk 말하다, 이야기하다
get(-got-gotten) 얻다
look …으로 보이다
handsome 잘생긴, 멋진
ask 요청하다, 묻다

say 말하다
must …해야 한다
play room 놀이방
wonderful 멋진
wish 바라다, 희망하다
look at …을 바라보다, 응시하다
each other 서로

Clown, who were you talking to?
광대야, 너 누구랑 이야기하고 있었니?

He looks so brave and handsome. Ask him to come here.
그는 잘생긴 데다가 정말 용감해 보여. 그에게 이리 오라고 해 봐.

🤡 Be careful, dancing doll. The Jack-in-the-box will be jealous.

👧 I don't care about the Jack-in-the-box. I don't like him.

🤡 Nobody likes him. But he is very strong. Everyone has to be careful around him.

👧 You're right. I'll be careful.

The dancing doll looked at the tin soldier and smiled. When he saw her smile, his heart felt warm and happy. He stood up straight, and smiled at the dancing doll.

Be careful 조심해
jealous 질투가 많은, 시샘하는
care about …에 마음쓰다
　　　　　…에 관심을 가지다
nobody 아무도 …않다
strong 강한
everyone 모든 사람

dancing doll 춤추는 인형
smile 미소, 웃음
heart 마음, 심장
feel(-felt-felt) warm 따뜻해지다
stand(-stood-stood) up straight
　똑바로 서다
smile at …에게 미소짓다

Everyone has to be careful around him.  모두가 그를 조심해야 해.

When he saw her smile, his heart felt warm and happy.
그가 그녀의 미소를 봤을 때 그의 심장은 따뜻해지고 행복으로
가득 찼습니다.

Suddenly, a large box burst open. The Jack-in-the-box jumped out of the box. The Jack-in-the-box was mean and angry.

Be quiet! You toys are making too much noise. I cannot sleep. Be quiet, I said.

Then he saw the tin soldier and the dancing doll.

Hey you, tin soldier. Quit looking at the dancing doll. She is mine. Did you hear me? I told you to quit looking at her.

You toys are making too much noise.
너희 장난감들은 너무 시끄러워.
Did you hear me?  내 말이 안 들려?

suddenly 갑자기, 별안간
a large 커다란, 큰
burst open 쾍 열리다, 왈칵 열다
jump out of …에서 뛰어나오다
mean 비열한
angry 화난, 성난
Be quiet! 조용히 해!
make a noise 떠들다, 떠들어대다

too much 너무 많은
sleep 잠자다
quit 그만 두다, 중지하다
look at …을 바라보다, 응시하다
mine 나의 것
hear 듣다
tell (-told-told) 말하다

Sir, I am a brave soldier. I must guard the play room. I will defend the dancing doll from you. I am not afraid of you.

You're not afraid of me? You will be. Wait until tomorrow. You will be afraid then.

The Jack-in-the-box went back into his box and slammed the lid. All the toys were quiet.

Oh, no. I was afraid of this. Now something terrible will happen.

I hope the tin soldier will be alright.

brave 용감한
guard 지키다, 수호하다
defend 방어하다, 지키다
afraid of 두려워하여, 무서워하여
wait 기다리다
until …까지

then 그 때는
slam (문을)쾅 닫다
lid 뚜껑
quiet 조용한
terrible 지독한, 끔찍한
alright(=all right) 무사한, 건강한

You're not afraid of me? You will be.
내가 두렵지 않다구? (하지만 곧)그렇게 될 걸.

I hope the tin soldier will be alright.
양철 병정에게 아무 일이 없길 바래.

# Comprehension

## Checkup I

### I  True or False

1. Johnnie lived with his parents in a big city.
2. One tin soldier only had one arm.
3. The tin soldier played with the other toys.
4. The dancing doll thought the tin soldier was handsome.
5. The dancing doll and the tin soldier talked to each other.

### II  Multiple Choice

1. How old was Johnnie on his birthday?
   a. He was six years old.
   b. He was sixteen years old.
   c. He was sixty years old.

2. Why did Johnnie's father want to take the tin soldier back to the store?
   a. To get his money back.
   b. To get a new one.
   c. To get a different toy.

3. What did Johnnie have to do before he went to bed?

   a. He had to put away his toys.
   b. He had to guard the play room.
   c. He had to brush his teeth.

4. Why didn't the tin soldier see the dancing doll's other leg?

   a. Because her other leg was high behind her back.
   b. Because her other leg was under her dress.
   c. Because she only had one leg.

5. Who were all the toys afraid of?

   a. They were all afraid of the tin soldier.
   b. They were all afraid of Johnnie.
   c. They were all afraid of the Jack-in-the-box.

# Comprehension
## Checkup I

**III** **Fill in the Blanks - use the words in the word bank**
(each word is used once)

| afraid | dances | down | felt | making |
| music | sleep | smile | terrible | woke |

1. He _____ up and ran _____ the stairs.

2. When her _____ plays, she _____ on her toes.

3. When he saw her _____, his heart _____ warm and happy.

4. You toys are _____ too much noise. I cannot _____.

5. I was _____ of this. Now something _____ will happen.

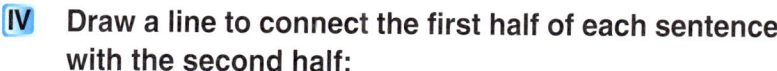

## IV  Draw a line to connect the first half of each sentence with the second half:

| A | B |
|---|---|
| The tin soldiers • | • knew everyone in the play room. |
| The teddy bears • | • were Johnnie's favorite toys. |
| The stuffed clown • | • was jealous and mean. |
| The dancing doll's dress • | • stole the zoo animals. |
| The Jack-in-the-box • | • had a silver star. |

## Chapter 3

The next morning, Johnnie woke up and ran into the play room.

 Come on, tin soldier. Let's have breakfast.

Johnnie grabbed the tin soldier and turned to the door. Suddenly, he tripped. The tin soldier flew out of his hand and out the window.

the next morning 이튿 날 아침
play room 놀이방
Come on 자, 가자
have breakfast 아침(밥)을 먹다

grab 부여잡다, 움켜쥐다
turn to 방향을 바꾸다, 향하다
trip 걸려 넘어지다
fly(-flew-flown) out 날아가다

Let's have breakfast. 아침 먹자.

Johnnie grabbed the tin soldier and turned to the door.
조니는 장난감 병정을 집어 들고 문으로 향했습니다.

Oh, no! My tin soldier!

Johnnie, what's the matter?

I wanted to take my tin soldier to breakfast. Then I tripped on the Jack-in-the-box. He flew out the window.

If you put your toys away, you would not trip on them. Let's go look for your soldier.

Stupid old Jack-in-the-box.

matter 문제, 일, 사건
take 데려가다
put away 치우다

look for 찾다
stupid 바보 같은, 어리석은

what's the matter? 무슨 일이니?

If you put your toys away, you would not trip on them.
네가 장난감들을 치워 놓았더라면 (장난감에) 걸려 넘어지는 일은 없었잖니?

Johnnie and his mother went to look for the tin soldier. They didn't hear the quiet laughter coming from the box. Unfortunately, as soon as they went outside, it began to rain.

 Oh, dear. Let's go back inside.

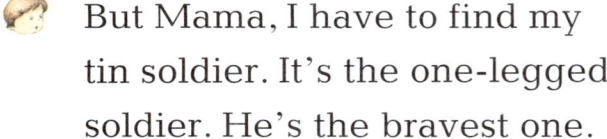 But Mama, I have to find my tin soldier. It's the one-legged soldier. He's the bravest one.

It's raining. You will catch a cold in the rain.

Please, Mama. I have to find him.

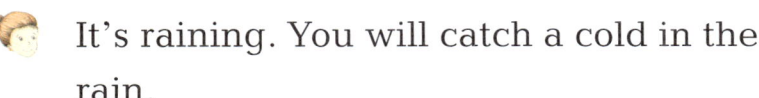 Don't worry. He will not go anywhere. We can look for him after it stops raining.

Oh, alright.

The Steadfast Tin Soldier

go(-went-gone) to ⋯하러 가다
laughter 웃음, 웃음 소리
come from ⋯에서 나오다
unfortunately 유감스럽게도
as soon as ⋯하자마자
go(-went-gone) outside
　밖으로 나가다
begin(-began-begun) to
　⋯하기 시작하다

Oh, dear (감탄사)어머, 이런
back inside 안으로 돌아가다
have to(=must) ⋯해야 한다
find(-found-found) 찾다
one-legged 다리가 하나인, 외다리의
bravest (brave의 최상급)가장 용감한
catch a cold 감기에 걸리다
Don't worry 걱정 마라
anywhere 어디에도

as soon as they went outside, it began to rain.
그들이 밖으로 나가자마자 비가 내리기 시작했습니다.

It's raining. You will catch a cold in the rain.
비가 오잖니. 빗 속에 있으면 감기 걸린단다.

It rained for a long time. The puddles were wide and deep. The tin soldier was wet and very sad.

 The Jack-in-the-box did this evil thing. How will I get back inside? Johnnie and his mother will find me. Until then, I must remember to be brave.

Two boys were walking down the street. They were playing in the mud and the puddles. One of them found the tin soldier.

for a long time 오랫 동안
puddle (빗물 등의)웅덩이
wide and deep 넓고 깊은
wet 젖은
sad 슬픈
evil 사악한

until then 그 때까지
remember 기억하다
walk down 걸어 내려오다
street 거리, 길
in the mud 진흙탕에서

How will I get back inside? 어떻게 다시 안으로 돌아가지?

Until then, I must remember to be brave.
그 때까지 내가 용감해져야 함을 잊어서는 안 돼.

🧒 Hey, look at this. I found a tin soldier.

👧 But he only has one leg. He looks stupid. Throw him away.

🧒 No, let's sail him in the gutter.

👧 Ok. I'll make a newspaper boat.

The boys made a newspaper boat and put it in the gutter. Then they put the tin soldier in the boat. The tin soldier did not like riding on the boat. But he stood up straight and brave.

look at …을 보다
look stupid 바보처럼 보이다
throw away 던져 버리다
sail (장난감 배를)띄우다
gutter 도랑
make(-made-made) 만들다

newspaper boat
　신문으로 만든 종이배
riding on the boat 배에 타는 것
stand(-stood-stood) up straight
　똑바로 서다
brave 용감한

The tin soldier did not like riding on the boat. But he stood up straight and brave. 장난감 병정은 배에 타는 것을 좋아하지 않았지만 꿋꿋이 용감하게 서 있었습니다.

 Off you go, tin soldier.

Wow, look at him go!

The boat sailed down the gutter. There was lots of rain water, so the boat sailed very quickly. It bumped and turned in the gutter. It spun around and almost tipped over. The tin soldier was very nervous, but he stood straight and still.

 Where am I going? I must always remember to be brave. I will think of the dancing doll. I will be brave for her.

---

There was lots of rain water, so the boat sailed very quickly.
빗물이 많이 고여 있어서 배는 매우 빨리 떠내려갔습니다.
I will be brave for her. 그녀를 위해서 용감해질 거야.

Off you go 자, 가라
sail 항해하다, 떠내려가다
lots of 많은, 다수의
rain water 빗물
bump 부딪치다, 충돌하다

spin(-spun-spun) around
　빙글 돌다
almost 거의
tip over 뒤집어지다
nervous 두려워하는, 불안한

# Comprehension
## Checkup II

**I**  **True or False**

1. The tin soldier flew out the window.
2. It rained for a short time.
3. The tin soldier wanted to get back inside.
4. The tin soldier enjoyed riding in the boat.
5. The boat tipped over in the gutter.

**II**  **Multiple Choice**

1. What did Johnnie trip on?
    a. He tripped on the stuffed clown.
    b. He tripped on the tin soldier.
    c. He tripped on the Jack-in-the-box.

2. Where did Johnnie want to take the tin soldier?
    a. He wanted to take him to breakfast.
    b. He wanted to take him outside.
    c. He wanted to take him on a boat.

정답은 p.105에

3. What were the two boys doing?

   a. They were looking for toys.
   b. They were walking home.
   c. They were playing in the mud and the puddles.

4. What did the boys make for the tin soldier?

   a. They made a tin boat.
   b. They made a newspaper boat.
   c. They made a wooden boat.

5. Why did the boat sail quickly?

   a. Because there was lots of rain water.
   b. Because there was lots of wind.
   c. Because there were lots of newspapers in the gutter.

# Comprehension

## Checkup II

**III** **Fill in the Blanks - use the words in the word bank**
(each word is used once)

| began | door | grabbed | must | nervous |
| put | remember | soon | straight | trip |

1. Johnnie _____ the tin soldier and turned to the _____.

2. If you _____ your toys away, you would not _____ on them.

3. As _____ as they went outside, it _____ to rain.

4. The tin soldier was very _____, but he stood _____ and still.

5. I _____ always _____ to be brave.

**IV** **Draw a line to connect the first half of each sentence with the second half:**

| A | | B |
|---|---|---|
| The Jack-in-the-box wanted | • • | to find the tin soldier. |
| Johnnie wanted | • • | to sail the tin soldier in the gutter. |
| Johnnie's mother wanted | • • | to go inside when it started to rain. |
| The two boys wanted | • • | to be brave for the dancing doll. |
| The tin soldier wanted | • • | to get rid of the tin soldier. |

# Chapter 4

There the rain water washed the boat into the sewers. It was dark in the sewers, and it smelled very bad. All the garbage from the streets was in the sewers.

 Where am I going now? I am not a sailor. I am a soldier. I hope the dancing doll is safe.

The boat turned down a tunnel in the sewers. A rat was standing in the tunnel.

Then the rain water washed the boat into the sewers.
그리고 종이배는 빗물에 떠밀려 하수구로 떠내려갔습니다.
Where am I going now? 내가 지금 어디로 가는 거지?

wash 휩쓸어 가다
sewer 하수구
dark 어두운
smell bad 악취가 나다
　　　　　냄새가 고약하다
garbage 쓰레기

sailor 선원, 뱃사람
safe 안전한
turn down 내려가다
tunnel 터널
rat 들쥐

🐭 Hey, you. Stop right there. You need a pass to come here. Where is your pass?

🎩 I don't have a pass.

🐭 Then you can't come here. Stop your boat.

🎩 I can't stop the boat. I don't know how to sail.

🐭 Stop your boat, or I will arrest you.

right there 바로 거기
need 필요하다
pass 통행증

how to sail
어떻게 (배를)조종하는지
arrest 체포하다

You need a pass to come here.  여기 오려면 통행증이 있어야 해.
Stop your boat, or I will arrest you.  배를 멈추지 않으면 널 체포하겠다.

But the boat did not stop. It sailed down the tunnel.

Help! Help! He's getting away. He does not have a pass.

More rats came out. They chased the tin soldier and his boat. They jumped into the water and tried to stop the boat. But the water was too strong. The boat sailed away from the rats in the sewers.

get away 달아나다
come out 나오다
chase 뒤쫓다, 추적하다

jump 뛰어들다
try to …하려고 하다

They jumped into the water and tried to stop the boat. But the water was too strong.  그들은 물 속으로 뛰어들어 배를 멈추려고 했지만 물살이 너무 세찼습니다.

Soon, the tin soldier saw daylight ahead. The boat sailed out of the sewers. Now, he was on a river. He also heard a strange roaring sound.

 Where am I going now? I'm happy that I am out of the sewers. I can see the trees and the sky. But what is that strange sound?

Then the tin soldier saw what was making the strange sound. The boat was sailing towards a waterfall.

 Oh, no! I can't steer the boat to shore, and I can't stop it. I will go over the waterfall. I must remember to be brave.

see(-saw-seen) 보다
daylight 햇빛
ahead 앞쪽에
strange 이상한, 묘한
roaring 으르렁거리는, 울리는
sound 소리

towards …쪽으로, …을 향하여
waterfall 폭포
steer 조종하다
shore 물가, 강기슭
go over 건너다, 넘다

Soon, the tin soldier saw daylight ahead.
곧 장난감 병정은 앞쪽에서 햇빛이 비치는 것을 보았습니다.

Then the tin soldier saw what was making the strange sound.
그 때, 장난감 병정은 그 이상한 소리가 어디서 나는지 봤습니다.

The newspaper boat went over the waterfall. It filled up with water and sank into the ocean. The tin soldier fell over and over in the water. Then he landed on the bottom of the ocean.

 This is terrible. How will I get back home? I will never see the dancing doll again. I miss her so much.

fill up with …으로 가득 차다
sink(-sank-sunk) 가라앉다
the ocean 바다
fall(-fell-fallen) over 떨어지다
land (땅에)닿다, 착륙하다

bottom 바닥
terrible 끔찍한, 터무니없는
miss 보고 싶어하다
　　　 섭섭하게 여기다

It filled up with water and sank into the ocean.
배는 물이 가득 차더니 바다 속으로 가라앉았습니다.

Then he landed on the bottom of the ocean.
얼마 후 그는 바다 밑바닥에 닿았습니다.

Just then, a big fish swam up to the tin soldier.

Who are you? What are you doing here?

I am a tin soldier. Some boys put me in a boat. The boat sailed through the sewers. Then it sailed down a river. Then it went over a waterfall. When it sank, I landed here.

Lucky me! I am hungry, and you look delicious.

I am a brave soldier.
I am not afraid of you.
I will fight you.

You can try to fight me, little tin soldier. But I am much bigger than you.
I will eat you for my breakfast.

just then 바로 그때
swim(-swam-swum) up
  헤엄쳐 다가오다
through the sewers
  하수구를 통해
lucky me! 잘됐다, 다행이다

hungry 배고픈
look delicious 맛있어 보이다
be afraid of …을 두려워하다
fight 싸우다
much bigger than …보다 더 큰

Lucky me! I am hungry, and you look delicious.
잘됐군! 마침 배가 고프던 참이었는데 너 참 맛있어 보이는구나.

But I am much bigger than you. 하지만 내가 너보다 훨씬 더 큰 걸.

The tin soldier raised his gun and tried to shoot the big fish. But his gun did not work under water. The big fish opened its mouth and ate the tin soldier.

 This is even worse than the boat. It is dark in here. I cannot see, and I cannot move. But I will be brave. The dancing doll will be proud of me.

The big fish swam in the ocean. He swam up and down, and side to side. The tin soldier was dizzy inside the fish.

raise 올리다
shoot (총을)쏘다
work 작동하다
under water 물 속에서
eat(-ate-eaten) 먹다
even worse 더욱 나쁜

move 움직이다
be proud of …을 자랑스러워하다
up and down 위아래로
side to side 좌우로
dizzy 어지러운

This is even worse than the boat. 여기는 배보다 더 (상황이)안 좋군.

He swam up and down, and side to side.
큰 물고기는 위아래로, 좌우로 헤엄쳤습니다.

Suddenly, the fish stopped swimming. The tin soldier did not know it, but a fisherman caught the fish.

- Wow! Hey, Charlie, look at this fish. He's so big!
- He's the biggest fish we ever caught!
- He's heavy too.
- He will get a good price at the fish market.
- Maybe we will have him for lunch today.
- No, he's too big. He can feed a whole family. Let's sell him.

He's the biggest fish we ever caught!
이건 우리가 이제까지 잡은 것 중에서 가장 큰 물고기야!
He can feed a whole family.  온 가족이 먹을 수 있겠어.

stop swimming 헤엄을 멈추다
fisherman 어부
catch(-caught-caught) 잡다
ever (비교급·최상급과 함께)이제까지
heavy 무거운
good price 좋은 가격

fish market 어시장
maybe 아마도
lunch 점심 식사
feed 먹이다, 부양하다
whole family 온 가족
sell 팔다

The fishermen took the fish to the fish market. Their baskets were full of many fish. They opened their baskets and called to the shoppers.

Fresh fish! Fresh fish! Just caught this morning! Have a delicious fish dinner tonight! Get your fresh fish!

How much are your fish?

Two dollars a pound, ma'am.

This is a big fish here.

Yes, ma'am. He's the biggest fish we ever caught.

Their baskets were full of many fish.
그들의 바구니는 생선들로 가득 차 있었습니다.
Get your fresh fish! 싱싱한 생선 사세요!
How much are your fish? 생선은 얼마인가요?

take(-took-taken) 가져가다
basket 바구니
be full of …이 많다[가득 차다]
call to 소리치다
shopper 물건 사는 사람

fresh 싱싱한, 신선한
just 이제 방금, 막
tonight 오늘 밤
How much? 얼마인가요?
ma'am (부인의 호칭)아주머니, 부인

- I am cooking for guests tonight. We need a big fish for dinner.
- I'll give you a special price for him. He will be delicious.
- Thank you. Here is your money.
- Thank you, ma'am. Have a good day.
- Oh, he's so heavy.
- Do you need help?
- No, I'm fine. Thank you.

cook 요리하다(동사), 요리사(명사)
guest 손님
for dinner 저녁 식사감으로
special price 특별가

Have a good day
좋은 하루 되세요
so heavy 매우 무거운
I'm fine 괜찮아요

I'll give you a special price for him.
이 생선을 특별가로 드리리다.

Do you need help? 도와 드릴까요?

The cook took the fish away. The fish rocked back and forth in the cook's basket. The tin soldier rocked back and forth in the fish.

 Where are we going now? I cannot hear very well inside the fish. But if I am brave, I will be alright.

take(-took-taken) away 가져가다  back and forth 앞뒤로, 이리저리
rock 흔들리다, 진동하다  alright(=all right) 무사한, 건강한

The fish rocked back and forth in the cook's basket.
생선은 요리사의 바구니 속에서 앞뒤로 흔들렸습니다.

I cannot hear very well inside the fish.
물고기 뱃속에 있으니 잘 들을 수가 없군.

# Comprehension

## Checkup III

### I  True or False

1. The tin soldier was also a sailor.
2. A waterfall was making the roaring sound.
3. The fish was bigger than the tin soldier.
4. The fishermen decided to eat the big fish for lunch.
5. The cook needed help to carry the fish.

### II  Multiple Choice

1. Why did the sewers smell bad?
    a. Because it was dark in the sewers.
    b. Because rain water was in the sewers.
    c. Because lots of garbage was in the sewers.

2. Who asked the tin soldier for a pass?
    a. A rat did.
    b. A fish did.
    c. A fisherman did.

정답은 p.106에

3. Why did the fish stop swimming?

   a. Because if fell asleep.

   b. Because a fisherman caught it.

   c. Because it went over a waterfall.

4. Where did the fishermen take the fish?

   a. They took it to the fish market.

   b. They took it to the cook's house.

   c. They took it to Namdaemun.

5. Why did the cook need a big fish?

   a. Because she was hungry.

   b. Because she was cooking for guests.

   c. Because she got a good price.

# Comprehension
## Checkup III

**III** **Fill in the Blanks - use the words in the word bank**
(each word is used once)

| away | biggest | ever | fell | forth |
| rats | right | rocked | water | you |

1. Hey, _____. Stop _____ there.

2. The boat sailed _____ from the _____ in the sewers.

3. The tin soldier _____ over and over in the _____.

4. He's the _____ fish we _____ caught.

5. The fish _____ back and _____ in the cook's basket.

The Steadfast Tin Soldier

**IV** **Draw a line to connect the first half of each sentence with the second half:**

| A | B |
|---|---|
| The rats jumped into the water | and ate the tin soldier. |
| The newspaper boat filled with water | and called to the shoppers. |
| The tin soldier raised his gun | and tried to stop the boat. |
| The big fish opened its mouth | and tried to shoot the big fish. |
| The fishermen opened their baskets | and sank into the ocean. |

# Chapter 5

Finally, the cook got home. She took the fish to the kitchen. She took a big, sharp knife and cut open the fish. Suddenly, the tin soldier fell out of the fish.

- Oh, my goodness! Look what I found.
- What is it?
- It's a little tin soldier. He was inside the fish.

finally 마침내, 드디어
get(-got-got) home 집에 도착하다
to the kitchen 부엌으로
sharp knife (날이)잘 드는 칼
cut 자르다

suddenly 갑자기
fall(-fell-fallen) out 빠져 나오다
Oh, my goodness! (감탄사)
   이런, 세상에
what I found 내가 뭘 발견했는지

She took a big, sharp knife and cut open the fish.
요리사는 크고 잘 드는 칼을 들고 생선의 배를 갈랐습니다.

Oh, my goodness. Look what I found.
이런, 세상에. 내가 뭘 발견했는지 좀 봐.

 How strange. How did he get in the fish?

 I don't know. He's lucky we found him.

 He's only got one leg. He's not always lucky.

 Don't say mean things like that. Let's clean him up. Then I will show him to Mrs. Smith.

The cook and the maid cleaned up the tin soldier. Soon, he was as good as new.

Don't say mean things like that.
그렇게 나쁘게 말하지 마.

Soon, he was as good as new.
그는 곧 새 것처럼 좋아졌습니다.

how (감탄문에서) 얼마나, 참으로
strange 이상한, 묘한
get in 들어가다
lucky 운 좋은
always 항상

mean 심술궂은
clean up 깨끗이 하다
show 보이다
as~ as… …처럼 ~한

The cook took him to the living room. Mr. and Mrs. Smith were there with their guests.

Madam, look what I found. This brave little soldier was inside a big fish.

Really? Let me see.

I know him. He is Johnnie's one-legged soldier.

You're right. We thought he was gone forever.

---

Really? Let me see. 정말인가요? 어디 봐요.

He is Johnnie's one-legged soldier.
이건 조니의 외다리 병정이잖소.

We thought he was gone forever.
우린 그가 영원히 사라진 줄 알았어요.

The Steadfast Tin Soldier

living room 거실
guest 손님
Madam (정중한 호칭)아씨, 부인
really 정말인, 사실인

one-legged 다리가 하나인, 외다리의
think(-thought-thought) 생각하다
be gone forever 영원히 사라지다

How did he get inside a fish?

Who knows? I'm sure he had many adventures.

If a fish ate me, I would die of fright.

Then he was very brave. Well done, soldier!

Johnnie will be so happy. This was his favorite tin soldier.

I will take it to him now. Please, excuse me.

Mrs. Smith went upstairs to the play room.

---

If a fish ate me, I would die of fright.
만일 물고기가 날 먹는다면 난 공포심에 죽고 말 거예요.

Mrs. Smith went upstairs to the play room.
스미스 부인은 위층 놀이방으로 올라갔습니다.

sure 확신하는, 확실한
adventure 모험, 진귀한 경험
eat(-ate-eaten) 먹다
die 죽다

fright 공포, 경악
Well done 잘했다, 훌륭하다
Excuse me 실례합니다
upstairs 위층으로, 계단을 올라서

Johnnie, I have something for you. Look.

It's my one-legged soldier. I looked everywhere. Where did you find him?

The cook found him in a fish.

Why was he in a fish?

I don't know. He had many adventures coming home.

something 어떤 것, 무엇인가
look 보다, 찾다
everywhere 어디에나, 도처에

find (-found-found) 찾다
cook 요리사

I have something for you. Look. 네게 줄 게 있단다. 보렴.

I looked everywhere. Where did you find him?
내가 모두 찾아봤는데. 그를 어디서 찾으셨어요?

Yes, the tin soldier was back home. He saw the stuffed clown. He saw the toy castle. And he saw the beautiful dancing doll. His heart was full of happiness. He smiled at the dancing doll, and she smiled at him. Then, an evil sound came from the Jack-in-the-box's box.

be back 돌아오다
see(-saw-seen) 보다
heart 마음, 가슴
be full of …이 많다[가득 차다]
happiness 행복, 기쁨

smile at …에게 미소를 짓다
evil sound 불길한 소리
come(-came-come) from
　…에서 (흘러)나오다

His heart was full of happiness.
그의 가슴은 기쁨으로 가득 찼습니다.

Then, an evil sound came from the Jack-in-the-box's box.
그때, 도깨비 인형이 들어 있는 상자에서 불길한 소리가 들려 왔습니다.

- I don't care. I don't want this stupid tin soldier anymore.

  Johnnie threw the tin soldier into the fireplace. Hot flames burned the brave, little tin soldier.

- Johnnie! Why did you throw your soldier into the fireplace? Now he is melting.

- I don't know. I just didn't want him anymore.

- That's no reason to destroy him. He was your favorite soldier.

- He's not my favorite. He's stupid.

- He is not stupid.
  He was very brave.
  Shame on you, Johnnie.

care 관심을 가지다, 상관하다
anymore (부정문에서)이제는, 더 이상
throw(-threw-thrown) 던지다
fireplace 벽난로
flame 불꽃, 화염

burn 태우다
melt 녹다
reason 이유, 까닭
destroy 파괴하다, 부수다
Shame on you 창피한 줄 알아라

Hot flames burned the brave, little tin soldier.
뜨거운 불길이 용감한 꼬마 병정을 덮쳤습니다.

That's no reason to destroy him.
그렇다고 장난감 병정을 없애 버릴 이유까지는 없잖니.

The fire in the fireplace was very hot.
The tin soldier was melting in the fire.
His gun was bending, and his paint was
burning off. But he stood up straight and
brave. He saw the dancing doll through
the flames.

fire 불길, 화염
bend 구부러지다, 휘다

paint 채색, 겉칠
burn off 타서 없어지다[벗겨지다]

The fire in the fireplace was very hot.
벽난로의 불길은 매우 뜨거웠습니다.

His gun was bending, and his paint was burning off.
그의 총은 휘어지고, (겉에 채색된) 칠은 타면서 벗겨져 갔습니다.

Dancing doll, I will be strong and brave for you. I love you.

My brave tin soldier, I will not let you die alone. I love you too.

Oh, no you don't. You are my dancing doll.

No, I'm not. I don't like you. You are mean and evil. I love the tin soldier.

let …하게 하다
alone 홀로, 외로이

mean 비열한, 심술궂은
evil 사악한

My brave tin soldier, I will not let you die alone.
나의 용감한 병정님, 당신을 홀로 죽게 하지는 않을 거예요.

Suddenly, a strong wind blew in through the window. The wind picked up the dancing doll. She spun in the air, and flew towards the fireplace. She landed in the fire next to the tin soldier. Soon, they both were gone.

strong wind 강풍
through the window
　창문을 통해서
pick up 들어올리다
spin(-spun-spun) 돌다
in the air 공중에서

fly(-flew-flew) 날다
towards …쪽으로, …을 향하여
land 닿다, 떨어지다
next to …의 옆에
be gone 사라지다

She spun in the air, and flew towards the fireplace.
그녀는 공중에서 빙글 돌더니 벽난로 쪽으로 날아갔습니다.

She landed in the fire next to the tin soldier.
그녀는 불 속의 장난감 병정 옆에 떨어졌습니다.

That night, the maid cleaned the fireplace. She found a small tin heart in the ashes. The silver star from the dancing doll's dress was melted into the heart. Now, the brave tin soldier and the beautiful dancing doll were together forever.

| | |
|---|---|
| that night 그날 밤 | ash 재 |
| maid 하녀 | melt 녹다 |
| tin heart 양철 하트 | together 함께 |
| clean 치우다, 청소하다 | forever 영원히 |

She found a small tin heart in the ashes.
하녀는 잿더미 속에서 조그만 양철 하트를 발견했습니다.

Now, the brave tin soldier and the beautiful dancing doll were together forever.  이제 용감한 장난감 병정과 아름다운 춤추는 인형은 영원히 하나가 되었습니다.

# Comprehension
## Checkup IV

### I  True or False

1. The cook found the tin soldier.
2. The maid said the tin soldier was not always lucky.
3. Mr. Jones thought the tin soldier was afraid.
4. The Jack-in-the-box was happy to see the tin soldier.
5. The tin soldier told the dancing doll that he loved her.

### II  Multiple Choice

1. Who did the cook show the tin soldier to?
   a. She showed him to Johnnie.
   b. She showed him to Mrs. Smith.
   c. She showed him to the dancing doll.

2. How did Mr. and Mrs. Smith feel when they saw the tin soldier?
   a. They were happy.
   b. They were angry.
   c. They were afraid.

3. **What did Johnnie do with the tin soldier?**

   a. He put him in a box.

   b. He threw him in the fireplace.

   c. He put him next to the dancing doll.

4. **Why did the dancing doll want to die with the tin soldier?**

   a. Because she loved the tin soldier.

   b. Because she loved the Jack-in-the-box.

   c. Because she was crazy.

5. **What did the maid find in the fireplace?**

   a. She found the tin soldier.

   b. She found the dancing doll.

   c. She found a tin heart.

# Comprehension

## Checkup IV

**III** **Fill in the Blanks - use the words in the word bank**
(each word is used once)

| anymore | ate | cut | favorite | fright |
|---------|-----|-----|----------|--------|
| reason | sharp | through | want | wind |

1. She took a big, _____ knife and _____ open the fish.

2. If a fish _____ me, I would die of _____.

3. I don't _____ this stupid tin soldier _____.

4. That's no _____ to destroy him. He was your _____ soldier.

5. Suddenly, a strong _____ blew in _____ the window.

The Steadfast Tin Soldier

**IV** **Draw a line to connect the words that are opposites of each other:**

| A | B |
|---|---|
| Day | Together |
| Afraid | Terrible |
| Wonderful | Outside |
| Inside | Night |
| Alone | Brave |

## Comprehension Checkup

### Checkup I (32~35p)

**I**  1. T   2. F   3. F   4. T   5. F

**II** 1. a   2. b   3. c   4. a   5. c

**III** 1. woke, down   2. music, dances
3. smile, felt   4. making, sleep
5. afraid, terrible

| A | B |
|---|---|
| The tin soldiers | knew everyone in the play room. |
| The teddy bears | were Johnnie's favorite toys. |
| The stuffed clown | was jealous and mean. |
| The dancing doll's dress | stole the zoo animals. |
| The Jack-in-the-box | had a silver star. |

**IV** Matching:
- The tin soldiers — were Johnnie's favorite toys.
- The teddy bears — knew everyone in the play room.
- The stuffed clown — stole the zoo animals.
- The dancing doll's dress — had a silver star.
- The Jack-in-the-box — was jealous and mean.

The Steadfast Tin Soldier

## Comprehension Checkup

**Checkup II** (48~51p)

I   1. T    2. F    3. T    4. F    5. F

II  1. c    2. a    3. c    4. b    5. a

III  1. grabbed, door    2. put, trip
     3. soon, began       4. nervous, straight
     5. must, remember

| A | B |
|---|---|
| IV The Jack-in-the-box wanted | to find the tin soldier. |
| Johnnie wanted | to sail the tin soldier in the gutter. |
| Johnnie's mother wanted | to go inside when it started to rain. |
| The two boys wanted | to be brave for the dancing doll. |
| The tin soldier wanted | to get rid of the tin soldier. |

Matching (per lines in image):
- The Jack-in-the-box wanted → to get rid of the tin soldier.
- Johnnie wanted → to sail the tin soldier in the gutter.
- Johnnie's mother wanted → to go inside when it started to rain.
- The two boys wanted → to find the tin soldier.
- The tin soldier wanted → to be brave for the dancing doll.

## Comprehension Checkup

## Checkup III (74~77p)

**I**  1. F   2. T   3. T   4. F   5. F

**II** 1. c   2. a   3. b   4. a   5. b

**III**
1. you, right
2. away, rats
3. fell, water
4. biggest, ever
5. rocked, forth

**IV**

| A | B |
|---|---|
| The rats jumped into the water | and ate the tin soldier. |
| The newspaper boat filled with water | and called to the shoppers. |
| The tin soldier raised his gun | and tried to stop the boat. |
| The big fish opened its mouth | and tried to shoot the big fish. |
| The fishermen opened their baskets | and sank into the ocean. |

The Steadfast Tin Soldier

## Comprehension Checkup

### Checkup IV (100~103p)

I  1. T    2. T    3. F    4. F    5. T

II  1. b    2. a    3. b    4. a    5. c

III  1. sharp, cut      2. ate, fright
    3. want, anymore    4. reason, favorite
    5. wind, through

IV

| A | B |
|---|---|
| Day | Together |
| Afraid | Terrible |
| Wonderful | Outside |
| Inside | Night |
| Alone | Brave |

## Word List

다음은 이 책에 나오는 단어와 숙어를 수록한 것입니다.
* 표는 중학교 영어 교육 과정의 기본 어휘입니다.

### A

| | |
|---|---|
| adventure | 85 |
| afraid of | 31 |
| ahead* | 59 |
| all day long | 15 |
| almost* | 47 |
| alone* | 95 |
| alright | 17 / 31 / 73 |
| always* | 81 |
| angry* | 29 |
| animal* | 17 |
| anymore | 91 |
| anywhere | 41 |
| arrest | 55 |
| as soon as | 41 |
| ash | 99 |
| ask* | 25 |
| as~ as… | 81 |

### B

| | |
|---|---|
| back* | 23 |
| back and forth | 73 |
| back inside | 41 |
| ballerina | 23 |
| ballet dress | 23 |
| bang | 17 |
| basket | 69 |
| be afraid of | 23 / 63 |
| be back | 89 |
| Be careful | 27 |
| be full of | 69 / 89 |
| be gone | 97 |
| be gone forever | 83 |
| be in love with | 23 |
| be proud of | 65 |
| Be quiet! | 29 |
| bed time | 17 |
| begin to | 41 |
| behind* | 23 |
| bend | 93 |

The Steadfast Tin Soldier

| | |
|---|---|
| birthday* | 11 |
| bottom* | 60 |
| brave | 21 / 23 / 31 / 45 |
| bravest | 15 / 41 |
| brush one's teeth | 17 |
| bump | 47 |
| burn* | 91 |
| burn off | 93 |
| burst open | 29 |

### C

| | |
|---|---|
| call to | 25 / 69 |
| care* | 91 |
| care about | 27 |
| careful | 23 |
| catch* | 67 |
| catch a cold | 41 |
| chase | 57 |
| clean* | 99 |
| clean up | 81 |
| clown | 19 |
| come from | 41 / 89 |
| Come on | 17 / 37 |
| come out | 57 |
| cook* | 71 / 87 |
| cut* | 79 |

### D

| | |
|---|---|
| dance* | 21 |
| dancing doll | 27 |
| dark* | 53 |
| daylight | 59 |
| defend | 31 |
| destroy | 91 |
| die* | 85 |
| dizzy | 65 |
| doll | 21 |
| Don't worry | 41 |

### E

| | |
|---|---|
| each other | 25 |
| eat* | 65 / 85 |
| even worse | 65 |
| ever* | 67 |
| everyone | 21 / 27 |
| everywhere | 87 |
| evil | 43 / 95 |
| evil sound | 89 |
| Excuse me | 85 |

### F

| | |
|---|---|
| fall out | 79 |

| | |
|---|---|
| fall over | 60 |
| favorite | 15 |
| feed* | 67 |
| feel warm | 27 |
| fight* | 17 / 63 |
| fill up with | 60 |
| finally* | 17 / 79 |
| find* | 41 / 87 |
| fire* | 93 |
| fireplace | 91 |
| fish market | 67 |
| fisherman | 67 |
| flame | 91 |
| fly* | 97 |
| fly out | 37 |
| for a long time | 43 |
| for dinner | 71 |
| forever | 99 |
| fresh* | 69 |
| fright | 85 |

### G

| | |
|---|---|
| garbage | 53 |
| get* | 15 / 25 |
| get away | 57 |
| get home | 79 |
| get in | 81 |
| go outside | 41 |
| go over | 59 |
| go to | 41 |
| go to sleep | 19 |
| Good morning | 11 |
| good price | 67 |
| grab | 37 |
| great* | 13 |
| guard | 17 / 31 |
| guest | 71 / 83 |
| gutter | 45 |

### H

| | |
|---|---|
| handsome | 25 |
| happen* | 21 |
| happiness | 89 |
| Have a good day | 71 |
| have breakfast | 37 |
| have to | 17 / 41 |
| hear* | 29 |
| heart* | 27 / 89 |
| heavy* | 67 |
| here you are | 13 |
| hit* | 17 |
| Hooray! | 17 |
| how* | 81 |
| How much? | 69 |

| | |
|---|---|
| how to sail | 55 |
| hungry* | 63 |
| hurt* | 15 |

### I

| | |
|---|---|
| I'm fine | 71 |
| in the air | 97 |
| in the mud | 43 |
| in the war | 15 |
| introduce | 19 |
| It is time to | 17 |

### J

| | |
|---|---|
| jack-in-the-box | 23 |
| jealous | 23 / 27 |
| job* | 19 |
| jump* | 57 |
| jump out of | 29 |
| just* | 13 / 69 |
| just then | 63 |

### K

| | |
|---|---|
| know* | 21 |

### L

| | |
|---|---|
| land* | 60 / 97 |
| large* | 29 |
| late* | 17 |
| laughter | 41 |
| leg* | 15 |
| let* | 95 |
| lid | 31 |
| little | 11 |
| live with | 11 |
| living room | 83 |
| look* | 25 / 87 |
| look at | 25 / 29 / 45 |
| look delicious | 63 |
| look for | 39 |
| look like | 21 |
| look stupid | 45 |
| lots of | 47 |
| lucky | 81 |
| lucky me! | 63 |
| lunch* | 67 |

### M

| | |
|---|---|
| ma'am* | 69 |
| Madam | 83 |
| maid | 99 |

| | |
|---|---|
| make* | 45 |
| make a noise | 29 |
| Mama | 11 |
| many* | 19 |
| matter | 39 |
| maybe* | 67 |
| mean* | 23 / 29 / 81 / 95 |
| melt | 91 / 99 |
| mine | 29 |
| miss* | 60 |
| move* | 65 |
| much bigger than | 63 |
| music* | 21 |
| must* | 25 / 43 |

### N

| | |
|---|---|
| need* | 55 |
| nervous | 47 |
| newspaper boat | 45 |
| next to | 97 |
| nobody | 27 |

### O

| | |
|---|---|
| Off you go | 47 |
| Oh, dear | 41 |
| Oh, my goodness! | 79 |
| once upon a time | 11 |
| one day | 11 |
| one-legged | 17 / 41 / 83 |
| open* | 13 |

### P

| | |
|---|---|
| paint | 93 |
| Papa | 11 |
| pass* | 55 |
| pick up | 97 |
| play* | 21 |
| play room | 25 / 37 |
| play together | 19 |
| play with | 15 |
| present* | 13 |
| pretty* | 23 |
| puddle | 43 |
| put away | 39 |

### Q

| | |
|---|---|
| question* | 21 |
| quiet* | 19 / 31 |
| quit* | 29 |

The Steadfast Tin Soldier

## R

| | |
|---|---|
| rain water | 47 |
| raise* | 65 |
| rat | 53 |
| really? | 83 |
| reason* | 91 |
| remember* | 43 |
| riding on the boat | 45 |
| right* | 15 |
| right there | 55 |
| roaring | 59 |
| rock* | 73 |
| run out of | 15 / 21 |
| run down | 11 |

## S

| | |
|---|---|
| sad* | 43 |
| safe* | 53 |
| sail | 45 / 47 |
| sailor | 53 |
| save* | 17 |
| say* | 25 |
| see* | 19 / 59 / 89 |
| sell* | 67 |
| sewer | 53 |
| Shame on you | 91 |
| sharp knife | 79 |
| shoot* | 65 |
| shopper | 69 |
| shore | 59 |
| show* | 81 |
| side to side | 65 |
| sink* | 60 |
| slam | 31 |
| sleep* | 29 |
| smell bad | 53 |
| smile* | 27 |
| smile at | 27 / 89 |
| so heavy | 71 |
| soldier* | 15 |
| something | 87 |
| sound* | 59 |
| special price | 71 |
| spin | 97 |
| spin around | 47 |
| stand* | 23 |
| stand up straight | 27 / 45 |
| start to | 19 |
| steal* | 17 |
| steer | 59 |
| stop swimming | 67 |
| strange* | 59 / 81 |
| street* | 43 |
| strong* | 21 / 27 |

| | |
|---|---|
| strong wind | 97 |
| stuff | 19 |
| stupid* | 39 |
| suddenly | 29 / 79 |
| sure* | 85 |
| swim up | 63 |

## T

| | |
|---|---|
| take* | 39 / 69 |
| take away | 73 |
| take back | 15 |
| talk* | 19 / 25 |
| teddy bear | 17 |
| tell* | 29 |
| terrible | 31 / 60 |
| that night | 99 |
| the next morning | 37 |
| the ocean | 60 |
| then* | 31 |
| think* | 83 |
| through the sewers | 63 |
| through the window | 97 |
| throw* | 91 |
| throw away | 45 |
| tin | 15 |
| tin heart | 99 |
| tinsmith | 15 / 21 |
| tip over | 47 |
| tip-toe | 23 |
| to the kitchen | 79 |
| to the store | 15 |
| today* | 13 |
| toe* | 21 |
| together* | 99 |
| tonight* | 69 |
| too much | 29 |
| towards* | 59 / 97 |
| toy | 15 |
| toy castle | 21 |
| trip* | 37 |
| true* | 23 |
| try to | 57 |
| tunnel | 53 |
| turn down | 53 |
| turn to | 37 |

## U

| | |
|---|---|
| under water | 65 |
| unfortunately | 41 |
| until then | 43 |
| until* | 31 |
| up and down | 65 |
| upstairs | 85 |

## W

| | |
|---|---|
| wait* | 15 / 31 |
| wake up | 11 / 19 |
| walk away | 25 |
| walk down | 43 |
| walk over | 19 |
| want to | 13 |
| war* | 17 |
| wash* | 53 |
| waterfall | 59 |
| wear* | 23 |
| welcome* | 19 |
| Well done | 85 |
| wet* | 43 |
| what I found | 79 |
| whole family | 67 |
| wide and deep | 43 |
| wish* | 25 |
| wonderful | 25 |
| work* | 65 |

## Y

| | |
|---|---|
| You're welcome | 13 |

## Z

| | |
|---|---|
| zoo* | 17 |

*Notes*

# THE STEADFAST TIN SOLDIER
**12** 장난감 병정

| | |
|---|---|
| **중쇄 펴낸날** | 2008년 3월 1일 |
| **펴낸이** | 강 남 현 |
| **펴낸곳** | 월드컴출판사 |
| **등록** | 2000년 1월 17일 |
| **주소** | 서울시 구로구 구로동 222-8 (우편번호 152-848) 코오롱 디지탈타워 빌란트Ⅱ 1005호 |
| **전화** | 02)3273-4300(대표) |
| **팩스** | 02)3273-4303 |
| **이메일** | wc4300@yahoo.co.kr |
| **홈페이지** | www.wcbooks.co.kr |

＊본 교재는 저작권법에 의해 보호를 받는 저작물이므로
　무단전재 및 무단복제를 금합니다.